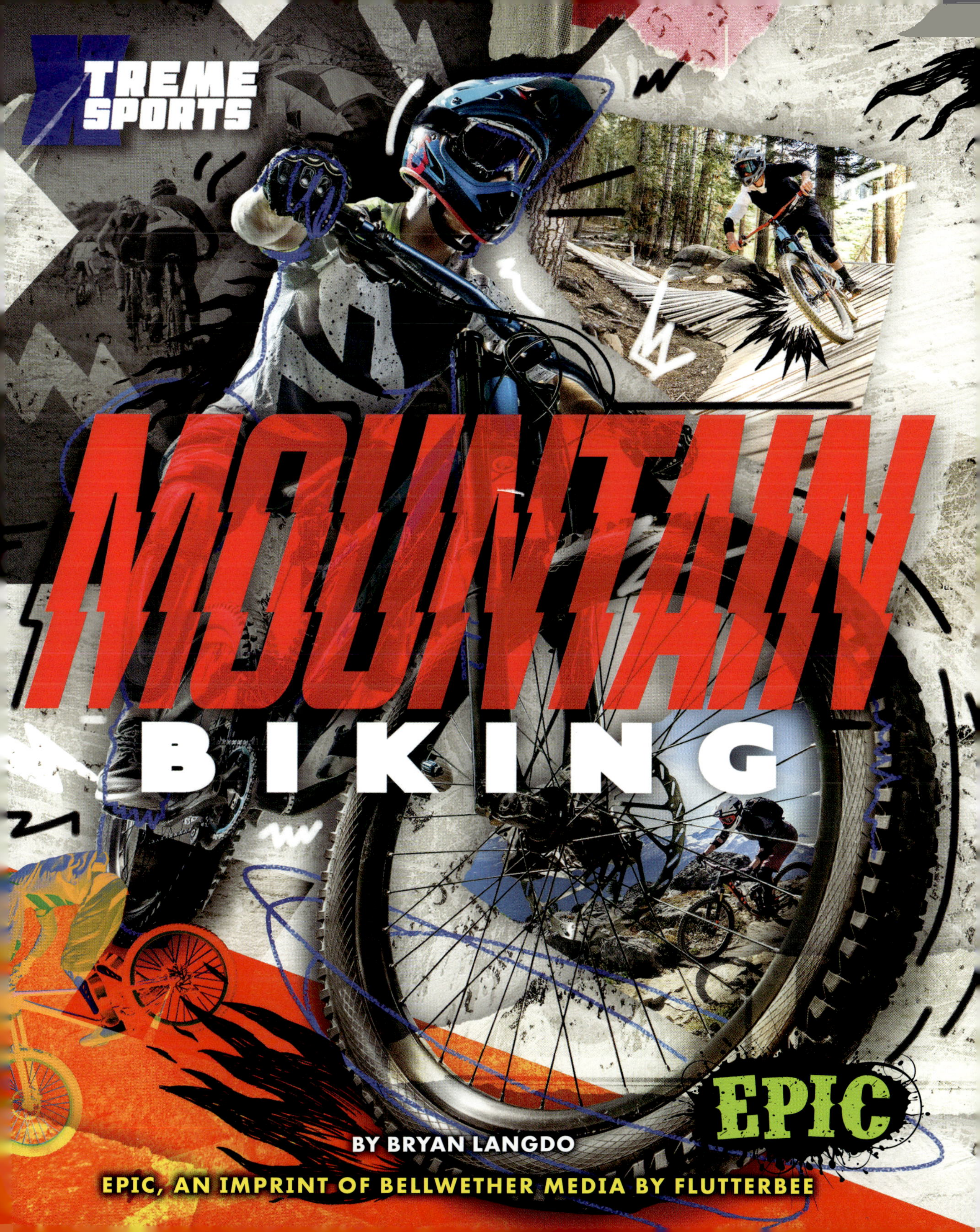

XTREME SPORTS

MOUNTAIN BIKING

EPIC

BY BRYAN LANGDO

EPIC, AN IMPRINT OF BELLWETHER MEDIA BY FLUTTERBEE

EPIC

EPIC BOOKS are no ordinary books. They burst with intense action, high-speed heroics, and shadows of the unknown. Are you ready for an Epic adventure?

This edition first published in 2027 by Bellwether Media, Inc.

For information regarding permission, write to Bellwether Media, Inc., Attention: Permissions Department, 3500 American Blvd W, Suite 150, Bloomington, MN 55431.

Library of Congress Cataloging-in-Publication Data is available at www.loc.gov or upon request from the publisher.

ISBN: 9798898800987 (hardcover)
ISBN: 9798898802226 (ebook)

Editor: Kieran Downs Designer: Jeffrey Kollock

Printed in the United States of America, North Mankato, MN.

TABLE OF CONTENTS

A ROCKY RIDE

A rider darts down a steep trail. His bike has thick tires. They glide over roots and rocks.

He makes a sharp turn. Dirt and pebbles fly. This is mountain biking!

SUPER SPEED

In 2022, Elias Schwärzler rode about 169 miles (272 kilometers) per hour on a mountain bike. It was a world record.

WHAT IS MOUNTAIN BIKING?

Mountain bikers ride bikes on trails and other off-road places.

MOUNTAIN BIKING GEAR

Some riders **compete** in long races. They ride up and down winding trails. Other riders prefer downhill races. They shoot down steep, rocky trails.

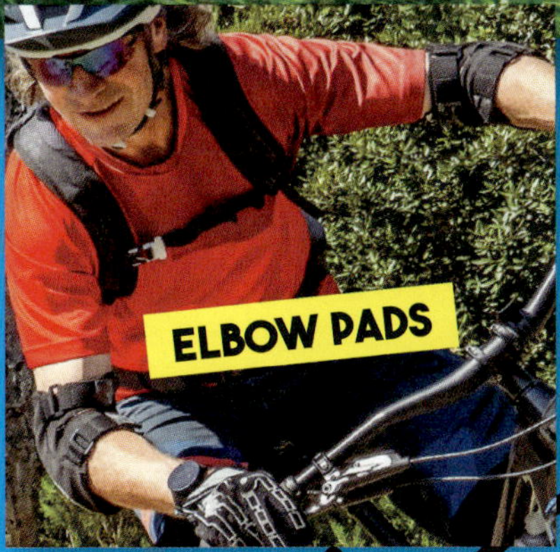

Mountain bikes are made for off-road riding. They have flat **handlebars**. Their tires have knobs. The knobs help the tires **grip** dirt.

Many mountain bikes have **suspension**. This makes a bumpy ride feel smoother.

FAMOUS LOCATION

MOAB

LOCATION	Utah, United States
FAMOUS FOR	Long and difficult trails through deserts, forests, and canyons

THE HISTORY OF MOUNTAIN BIKING

U.S. 25TH INFANTRY REGIMENT BICYCLE CORPS

People have ridden off-road bikes since the 1800s. The United States Army tested off-road bikes in the 1890s.

Modern mountain biking started in the late 1960s. Teenagers in California rode street bikes on trails.

TIMELINE

1890s The United States Army tests off-road bicycles

1976 Riders compete in the first Repack Race

RALEIGH

1985 The Raleigh bike company makes the first official mountain bike

IMBA

1988 The International Mountain Bicycling Association is formed

1996 Mountain biking becomes a Summer Olympic sport

Mountain biking grew more popular in the 1970s. People **modified** bikes. They added better brakes and tires. These bikes were called "klunkers."

In 1976, riders held a downhill race in California. It was called the Repack Race.

KLUNKERS USED IN A REPACK RACE

A LUCKY ONE

Alan Bonds was the only person to finish the first Repack Race without crashing. He was the winner.

A LONG RIDE

The Great Divide Mountain Bike Route is around 2,700 miles (4,345 kilometers) long. It goes from Canada to New Mexico.

GREAT DIVIDE ROUTE NEAR FERNIE, BRITISH COLUMBIA, CANADA

RALEIGH BIKE COMPANY FACTORY

In 1985, the Raleigh bike company made the first official mountain bike.

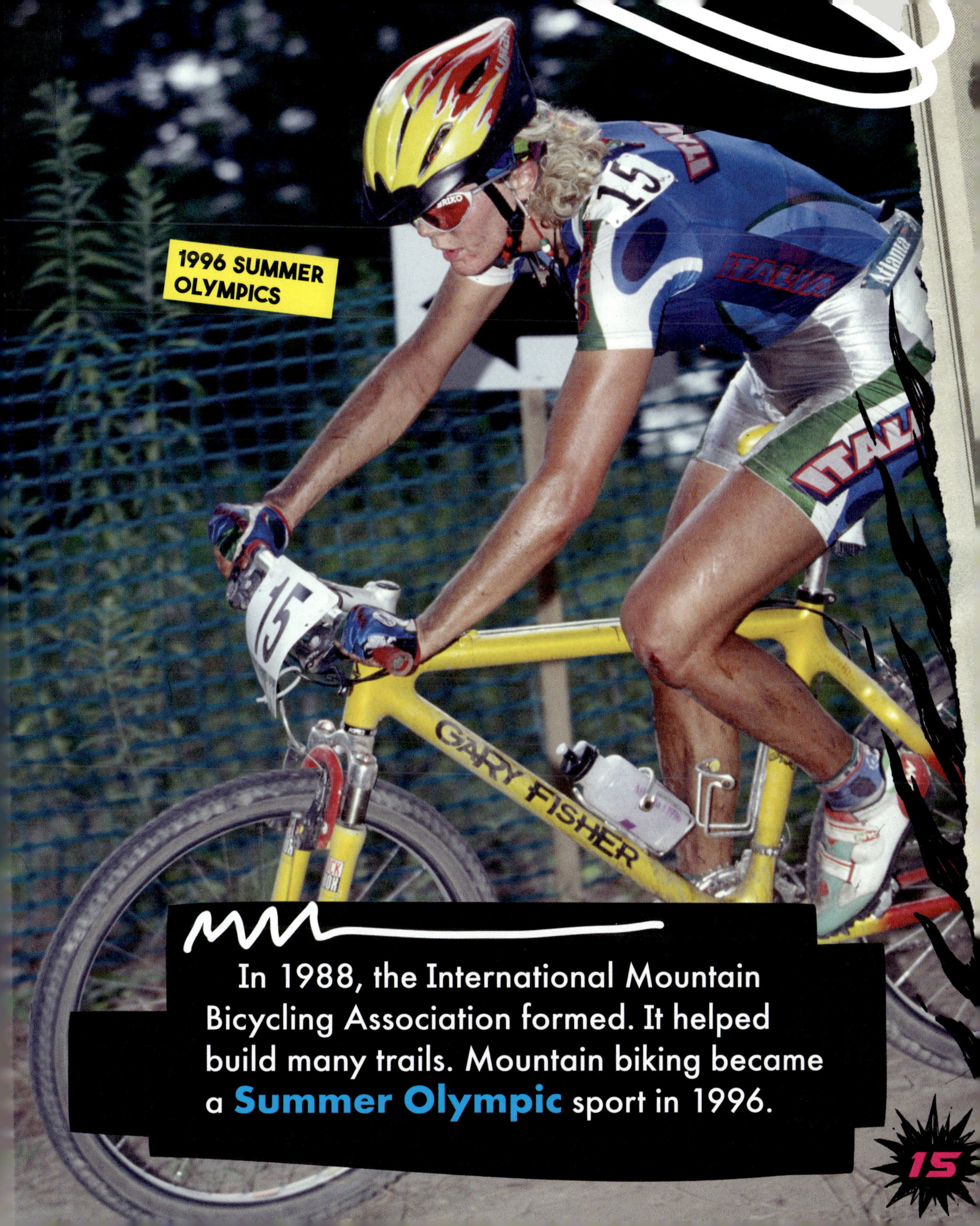

1996 SUMMER OLYMPICS

In 1988, the International Mountain Bicycling Association formed. It helped build many trails. Mountain biking became a **Summer Olympic** sport in 1996.

MOUNTAIN BIKING TODAY

Riders race on long courses in cross-country events. Riders take turns zipping down a track in downhill events. Whoever finishes the fastest wins.

In freeride events, riders zoom down hills. They score points for doing tricks.

HOW TO MANUAL

The Mountain Bike World **Championships** happen each year. Riders from around the world compete.

Red Bull Rampage is a freeride event for the world's best riders.

RED BULL RAMPAGE, 2024

MOUNTAIN BIKE WORLD CHAMPIONSHIPS, 2025

FAMOUS FACE

RACHEL ATHERTON

BIRTHDAY	December 6, 1987
HOMETOWN	Wells, United Kingdom
FAMOUS FOR	Winning many World Cup championships for downhill racing

Many people mountain bike for fun. Bike parks have trails and **obstacles**.

Some ski resorts have mountain bike trails in the summer. Ski lifts take riders up. It is fun to zoom down a mountain!

GLOSSARY

championships—contests to decide the best team or person

compete—to try to win something that someone else is also trying to win

grip—to hold without sliding

handlebars—bars riders hold onto that control a bike's direction

modified—made changes to something

obstacles—objects that add challenge to a path

Summer Olympic—related to a worldwide summer sports contest held in a different country every four years

suspension—the system on a bike that makes bumpy ground feel smoother for riders

TO LEARN MORE

AT THE LIBRARY

Gish, Ashley. *Cycling*. Mankato, Minn.: Creative Education and Creative Paperbacks, 2024.

Parker, Madison. *Going Mountain Biking*. Buffalo, N.Y.: Norwood House Press, 2026.

Troupe, Thomas Kingsley. *Mountain Bikes, Downhill*. Ann Arbor, Mich.: Cherry Lake Publishing Group, 2026.

ON THE WEB

FACTSURFER

Factsurfer.com gives you a safe, fun way to find more information.

1. Go to www.factsurfer.com.

2. Enter "mountain biking" into the search box and click .

3. Select your book cover to see a list of related content.

INDEX

The images in this book are reproduced through the courtesy of: Alex, front cover, p. 1; aaron, front cover, p. 1; Real Sports Photos, front cover, pp. 1, 3, 7 (knee pads), 16; Simona, front cover, pp. 1, 4, 5; anatoliy_gleb, p. 2; blas, p. 6; Yankovsky88, p. 6 (mountain bike); Halfpoint, p. 6 (helmet); Azee/ peopleimages.com, p. 6 (air pump); Davi Correa, p. 7; reisegraf.ch, p. 7 (elbow pads); Cast Of Thousands, p. 7 (water pack); baranq, p. 8; AC STUDIO, p. 8 (inset); Glevity, p. 9 (left); GROGL, p. 9 (right); Unknown/ Wikimedia Commons, p. 10; alexroch, p. 11; United States Geological Survey/ Wikimedia Commons, p. 12 (1890s); The AGE/ Getty Images, p. 12 (1996); Timothy Vollmer/ Flickr, p. 13; EMPICS Sport – EMPICS/ Getty Imaves, p. 14; Danita Delimont/ Alamy Stock Photo, p. 14 (inset); Graham Watson/ Getty Images, p. 15; LiveMedia, p. 16 (inset); Piotr Staron/ Getty Images, p. 18; Christian Pondella/ Getty Images, p. 18 (inset); Kay Roxby/ Alamy Stock Photo, p. 19 (left); martin SC photo, p. 19 (right); Fabio Averna/ Alamy Stock Photo, p. 19 (bottom); Ramon Cliff, p. 20; Michael J Magee, p. 20 (inset); Taras Hipp, p. 21; Almazoff, p. 21 (inset).